# How Molly Coddle Baked a School

by Kyle Mewburn

illustrated by Craig Smith

OXFORD
UNIVERSITY PRESS
AUSTRALIA & NEW ZEALAND

The Bunnabulla Town Fair was the most exciting event of the year. There were carnival rides and a huge street parade. But the most exciting event of all was the famous *Bunnabulla Bake-off*.

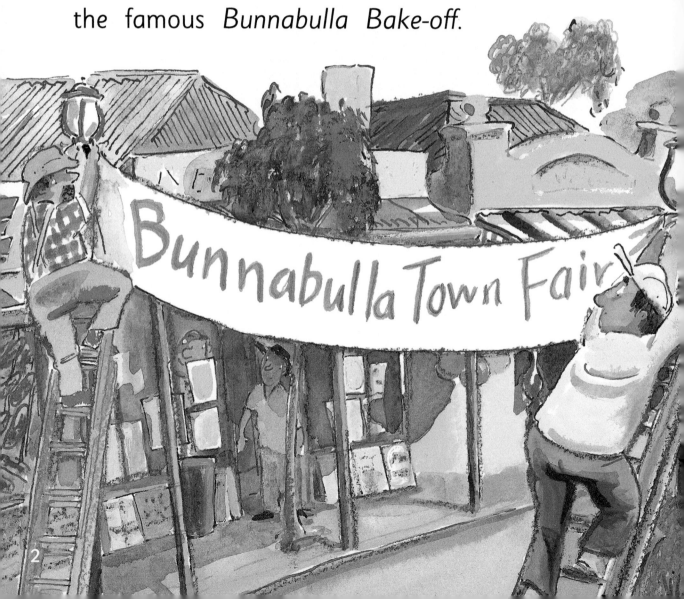

The winning cake, along with other goodies, was going to be donated to Bunnabulla's sister school in Thailand, which had been damaged by a monsoon.

Everyone wanted to win the *Bunnabulla Bake-off* and the fabulous first prize – a Palomino pony.

Molly Coddle really wanted that pony. There was only one problem: she couldn't bake.

3

Molly searched everywhere for the perfect cake recipe. Every time she thought she had a good one, she wrote it down.

But every time Molly thought she had the perfect recipe, she discovered the shop didn't have a vital ingredient — like rose water or elderflower syrup. So she had to start all over again.

Meanwhile, the day of the bake-off got closer.

One afternoon, while Molly was feeding the cows, she found an old recipe book buried under the hay. On the very first page was a recipe for "the simplest, most delicious chocolate ginger cake ever". It was perfect! She had all the ingredients, too.

Molly went straight to the kitchen. She mixed and grated and whipped and folded. She followed the recipe EXACTLY and then put the cake in the oven.

When the timer went off, Molly took the cake out right away and ... it wasn't perfect at all! The outside was burnt and the inside was gooey.

She gave it to the pigs, but even they wouldn't eat it.

Meanwhile, the day of the bake-off got closer.

The next day, Molly tried again. She mixed and grated and whipped and folded. She followed the recipe EXACTLY and then put the cake in the oven.

When the timer went off, Molly took the cake out right away and ... it still wasn't perfect! This time the inside was burnt and the outside was gooey.

She gave it to the chickens, but even they wouldn't eat it. And the bake-off was the next day!

That night, Molly sneaked into her dad's shed where there was an old oven. She didn't want anyone to know she wasn't in bed, so she didn't turn on the light. She used a head lamp instead.

One more time, Molly mixed and grated and whipped and folded. She followed the recipe EXACTLY and then put the cake in the oven. Then she fell asleep.

While Molly slept, the cake baked all night.

When she finally woke up, Molly took the cake out of the oven and, although it smelt a bit funny, it looked perfect! So she covered it with chocolate icing and then raced into town.

But when Molly reached the town hall, her heart sank. It was full of perfect cakes. Molly knew her cake would *never* win. Glumly, she went outside to watch the street parade.

While everyone was watching the street parade, a goat sneaked into the town hall. One by one, it ate all the cakes. But when the goat tried to eat Molly's cake, it nearly broke its teeth.

When the judges came back inside and saw the mess the goat had made, they were horrified. What would the people in Thailand think when they got a box full of cream and goo?

Then someone found Molly's cake. It was the only cake still in one piece! So Molly was declared the winner of the bake-off.

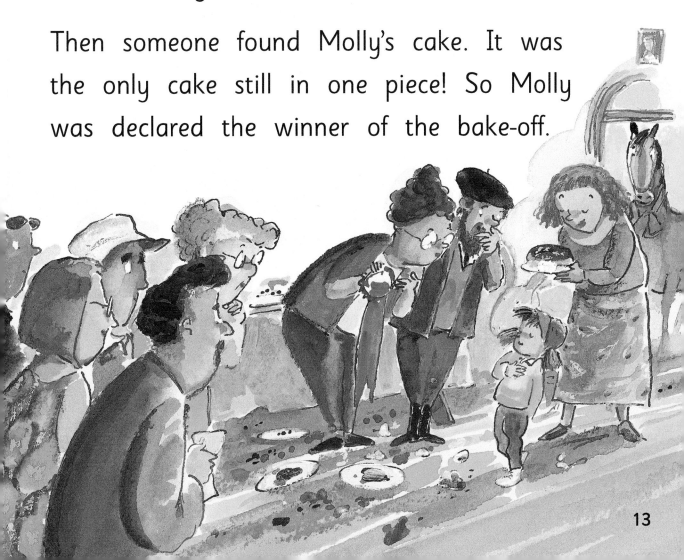

The people in Thailand were very disappointed when they got Molly's cake. It was so hard it nearly broke their teeth. They tried giving it to the pigs, but the pigs wouldn't eat it. So they tried giving it to the chickens, but the chickens wouldn't eat it, either. Then someone had a great idea.

They sent Molly a letter asking if she could bake a thousand more cakes just like her winning cake. Molly was flattered and got to work in the kitchen straight away.

She mixed and grated and whipped and folded. She followed the recipe EXACTLY.

But when she took the cake out of the oven, it was all burnt. Then she remembered she'd made her winning cake in her dad's shed.

When Molly went back to the shed, she found an open bag of cement. Now she realised why the goat hadn't eaten her cake – Molly had used cement instead of flour!

Molly baked all summer long, until she'd baked a thousand concrete cakes. Of course, the cakes were too hard to eat but they were perfect for bricks. And the bricks were used to rebuild the school in Thailand.

And that's how Molly Coddle baked a school!